CELEBRATING THE NAME EMILY

Celebrating the Name Emily

Walter the Educator

Silent King Books

Copyright © 2024 by Walter the Educator

All rights reserved. No part of this book may be reproduced in any manner whatsoever without written permission except in the case of brief quotations embodied in critical articles and reviews.

First Printing, 2024

Disclaimer
This book is a literary work; poems are not about specific persons, locations, situations, and/or circumstances unless mentioned in a historical context. This book is for entertainment and informational purposes only. The author and publisher offer this information without warranties expressed or implied. No matter the grounds, neither the author nor the publisher will be accountable for any losses, injuries, or other damages caused by the reader's use of this book. The use of this book acknowledges an understanding and acceptance of this disclaimer.

dedicated to everyone with the first name of Emily

EMILY

Emily, oh how thy name doth dance upon the lips,

A melody of syllables that in the mind do skips.

E
M
I
L
Y

A name so fair, so full of grace,

A tapestry of letters in a wondrous embrace.

In the garden of names, Emily blooms like a rose,

A name that in its elegance, everyone knows.

It whispers of strength, of beauty untold,

EMILY

In the symphony of names, it stands bold.

From the ancient hills to the modern streets,

E
M
I
L
Y

Emily's name echoes, never to retreat.

It carries a legacy, a story to be told,

EMILY

Of triumph and courage, a spirit so bold.

In the chambers of the heart, it resonates deep,

A name that in its essence, promises to keep.

A beacon of hope in the darkest of night,

Emily, a name that shines so bright.

Like the gentle stream, it flows with ease,

A name that brings comfort, a gentle breeze.

In every corner of the world, it finds its place,

A name that embodies love and grace.

Emily, a name that weaves dreams into reality,

A symphony of letters that ignites vitality.

In the tapestry of existence, it holds its own,

A name that in its uniqueness, has grown.

From the pages of history to the present day,

EMILY

Emily's name stands tall, in its own special way.

It paints a picture of resilience and art,

A name that etches itself in every heart.

So here's to Emily, in all her splendor,

A name that in its essence, is truly tender.

A name that sparkles, a name that gleams,

In the labyrinth of names, it reigns supreme.

Emily, a name of ancient lineage and lore,

Born from the whispers of time long before.

E
M
I
L
Y

It harks back to distant lands and tales of old,

A name with a history, a story to be told.

EMILY

In the annals of yore, it found its genesis,

A name that in its origins, holds mysteriousness.

From the emerald isles to the hills of yore,

Emily's roots run deep, forevermore.

ABOUT THE CREATOR

Walter the Educator is one of the pseudonyms for Walter Anderson. Formally educated in Chemistry, Business, and Education, he is an educator, an author, a diverse entrepreneur, and he is the son of a disabled war veteran. "Walter the Educator" shares his time between educating and creating. He holds interests and owns several creative projects that entertain, enlighten, enhance, and educate, hoping to inspire and motivate you.

> Follow, find new works, and stay up to date
> with Walter the Educator™
> at WaltertheEducator.com

www.ingramcontent.com/pod-product-compliance
Lightning Source LLC
LaVergne TN
LVHW010622070526
838199LV00063BA/5236